THE

⦁ORACLE

BOOK

*Answers to Life's
Questions*

GEORGIA ROUTSIS SAVAS

Illustrations by Melanie Marder Parks

SIMON & SCHUSTER
New York London Toronto Sydney Singapore

ALSO BY

GEORGIA ROUTSIS SAVAS

Total Astrology:
What the Stars Say About Life and Love

SIMON & SCHUSTER
Rockefeller Center
1230 Avenue of the Americas, New York, NY 10020

For information about special discounts for bulk purchases,
please contact Simon & Schuster Special Sales:
1-800-456-6798 or business@simonandschuster.com

SIMON & SCHUSTER and colophon are
registered trademarks of Simon & Schuster, Inc.

Designed by Bonni Leon-Berman
Illustrations copyright © 2001 by Melanie Marder Parks
Manufactured in the United States of America

1   3   5   7   9   10   8   6   4   2

Library of Congress Cataloging-in-Publication Data
Savas, Georgia Routsis.
The oracle book : answers to life's questions / Georgia Routsis Savas
p. cm.
1. Divination. 2. Oracles. I. Title.
BF1751 .S28 2001
133.3—dc21   2001034155
ISBN 0-7432-2187-7

ACKNOWLEDGMENTS

THIS BOOK OWES ITS EXISTENCE TO THE FOLLOWING FOLKS: To my editor, Amanda Murray, for her gracious guidance (and for instinctively pitching this project to me, the Queen of Divining). To Simon & Schuster, for putting this book together and for coming up with an extraordinary visual package. To Ruth Sullivan, the wise woman of publishing, for her help and expertise. To JR Watson, for his semi-rational assistance. To my grandmother, Anna Skunakis, who introduced me to soothsaying. To my parents, Gus and Stella Routsis, for supplying my genetic blueprint (for better or for worse). To Savannah, for her canine intuition. And to my husband, Damon, for his ironclad support, never-ending patience . . . and just about everything else.

INTRODUCTION "What should I do?" is a question that just about every living, breathing human being has asked at some point in his or her life. Some folks ask family and friends for advice, others seek guidance from a therapist, still others call upon a psychic or astrologer to illuminate the situation. No matter the method used in this world of I-wanted-it-yesterday, people want their answers delivered quickly. ∞ THERE ARE HUNDREDS, if not thousands, of divination techniques available that give pretty near instant answers. They range from the familiar, like Crystallomancy (using a crystal ball), to the more obscure, like Capnomancy (the study of smoke rising from a fire). By using *The Oracle Book* you'll be practicing a form of Bibliomancy—the answering of a question by means of randomly choosing a word or passage from a book. ∞ THOUGH THE BIBLE was historically the book of choice for Bibliomancy, people have also used ancient Greek epics, poetry or Shakespearean works. Many believe Bibliomancy is the Western world's answer to the *I Ching: The Book of Questions,* a divination system developed by the Chinese over four thousand years ago. When people consult the *I Ching,* they throw yarrow stalks or coins and interpret the way in which they fall as the answer to their question. ∞ NOWADAYS, MOST PEOPLE don't have yarrow stalks handy, or much patience to decipher cryptic messages. That's where *The Oracle Book* comes in. This handy do-it-yourself divination tool takes its name from the oracles of ancient Greece—these were humans who acted as divine intermediaries, delivering messages from the gods to their earthbound peers. But the term "oracle" can also refer to the message itself, a magical glimpse into the future, and that's how it's used here. *The Oracle Book* brings together a wealth of predictions drawn from a variety of ancient and modern divination techniques. Within these pages are predictions drawn from astrology, tarot cards, tea leaves, playing cards, dice, the crystal ball, palmistry and psychic wisdom. ∞ IN ORDER TO ☉ get started, first you're going to have to check your logic at the door and rely on your intuition. The truth is that Bibliomancy and other forms of divination aren't really about predicting the future. They are tools that can help guide you to the answer that already lies deep inside yourself. The answer you pick is determined by the exact moment you, and only you, decide to stop flipping through *The Oracle Book*. Somehow, the page with the "right" answer just beckons you to stop. ∞ THERE ARE SOME lucky people who already possess finely tuned intuitive skills. They're the ones who always seem to be in the right place at the right time. But if you're one of those highly evolved souls with a, hmm, "deeply buried intuition," don't despair. Chances are your inner guide is safe and sound. Have you ever turned on the radio to find that the song you've been humming all day happens to be on? Or run into an old acquaintance that you've been thinking about just minutes before? If so, you've got what it takes to get your intuition (back) in shape. All it needs is regular exercise, which is what you'll get by using this book.

HOW TO USE THE
ORACLE BOOK

Unlike other forms of divination, with *The Oracle Book* there's no in-depth studying required. No special incantation to memorize, no swami to venerate and no fancy fortune-telling outfit involved—all you need is a few minutes and an open mind. TO BEGIN, HOLD the book in both hands and take a few deep, cleansing breaths. Then concentrate on a yes-or-no question. When your question is clear in your mind, repeat it once (silently or aloud). Then run your thumb (your left if you're left-handed, right if you're right-handed) over the edge of the pages and when you sense your thumb is in the right place, open the book. The answer to your question will be revealed. SOMETIMES AN ANSWER will make immediate sense and will apply directly to you and your situation. Other times, the advice will seem vague. Pay attention to how you're feeling when you're submitting your query. An imprecise question (or unsure mind) invariably yields an unclear answer. Excuse the cliché, but in divining, practice does make perfect. The more you use this tool, the sharper your intuition gets. And therein lies the secret to finding the ever-elusive "right" answer.

THE
O·RACLE
BOOK

ASTROLOGY

THE MOON,
illuminary of
intuition,
counsels you
to rely on your
first impression.

TAROT

You've drawn the
KING OF
PENTACLES:
consult a
knowledgeable
authority.

PSYCHIC

Listen to the
PSYCHİC:
the time is right.

PALMISTRY

THE PALM READER

sees a cross in the palm,

which indicates

a challenge.

Rise to it.

TEA LEAVES

AT THE
BOTTOM
OF YOUR
CUP

is the shape
of a dolphin:
have fun with it.

CRYSTAL BALL

THE
CRYSTAL
BALL

shows a

setting sun:

time is

running out.

DİCE

THE DİCE

have come up

triple sixes:

smile,

there is every

indication

of happiness.

ASTROLOGY

MERCURY,
the planet of intellect,
advises you to
take the
next logical step.

DİCE

A ROLL OF NUMBER SEVENTEEN

means
success depends
on perseverance.

PLAYING CARD

You've drawn

THE FIVE OF

SPADES:

it will be tough.

TAROT

You've drawn
THE QUEEN OF
PENTACLES:
your prayers will be
answered.

PSYCHİC

THE PSYCHIC'S RESPONSE:

only if it will make
you happy.

PALMISTRY

THE PALM
READER

sees a trident shape

in the palm:

use a more

creative approach.

TEA LEAVES

AT THE BOTTOM
OF YOUR CUP
is the shape of a cat:
don't obsess about it
and it will
come to you.

CRYSTAL BALL

THE
CRYSTAL
BALL

reveals a bag of coins:

what you wish for

may cost you.

DICE

YOU'VE ROLLED NUMBER SIXTEEN:

as long as no hazard is involved.

ASTROLOGY

VENUS,
the planet of love,
urges you
to follow
your heart.

PLAYING CARD

You've selected
THE FOUR OF
SPADES:
you already
know the answer.

TAROT

You've drawn
THE PRINCE OF
PENTACLES:
tell it like it is.

PSYCHIC

THE PSYCHIC

counsels you

to act prudently.

PALMISTRY

THE PALM READER

sees a full mount

of Neptune:

you alone

cannot control

the outcome.

TAROT

You've drawn the
PRINCESS OF
PENTACLES:
you've already learned
your lesson.

TEA LEAVES

THE TEA
LEAVES

have formed a rose:
the line between
pain and pleasure
is obscured.

DICE

THE DİCE

have come up
triple fives:
only if you
change your
priorities.

PLAYING CARD

You've selected
THE QUEEN OF
DIAMONDS:
be careful what
you wish for.

PALMISTRY

THE PALM READER

sees a deep line
of Apollo:
a dazzling result
is forecast.

†EA LEAVES

THE TEA
LEAVES
have formed
the shape of a broom:
this is not the time
to be secretive.

CRYSTAL BALL

According to the
CRYSTAL
BALL,
it will bring
you good luck.

DİCE

YOU'VE ROLLED A FIVE:

providence supports
you as long as you
take care of
yourself.

ASTROLOGY

ΠΕΡΤ∩Ε,
the planet of illusion,
warns that you will
be deceived if
you follow through.

DİCE

YOU'VE ROLLED A FOUR:

someone will try to

prevent it

from happening.

CRYSTAL BALL

The image in

THE
CRYSTAL
BALL

warns you
to proceed
with caution.

PLAYING CARD

You've
selected
THE TEN OF
DIAMONDS:
be on your
guard.

PALMISTRY

THE PALM READER

sees a

frayed heart line,

which means

you need to

focus your

attentions.

TAROT

You've drawn
THE PRIƟCE
OF WAƟDS:
the winds of change
are blowing
your way.

PALMISTRY

THE PALM READER

sees a break

in the life line:

expect an

unexpected

outcome.

PSYCHİC

THE PSYCHIC

foresees

unexpected travel

related to

your question.

PLAYING CARD

You've drawn
THE NINE OF
DIAMONDS:
appreciate things
as they are.

CRYSTAL BALL

The image in

THE

CRYSTAL

BALL

is bright—

move forward

with your plans.

TEA LEAVES

THE TEA-LEAF READER

sees the shape

of an ant:

allow someone

to assist, and you will

achieve victory.

DİCE

YOU'VE ROLLED A THREE:

you will succeed according to your wish.

ASTROLOGY

PLUTO,
the planet of
transformation,
commands you
to forget about it.

DİCE

THE DİCE

indicate your
gain will be
significant.

PLAYING CARD

You've selected
THE EİGHꝉ OF
DİAMⲞⲚDS:
be more loving and you
will be rewarded.

CRYSTAL BALL

The image in
THE
CRYSTAL
BALL
is murky—ask
again later.

PALMISTRY

According to
THE PALM
READER,
the fate line shows
that no one can
prevent it from
happening.

PSYCHIC

THE
PSYCHİC

suggests you
think it
through.

TAROT

You've drawn
THE PRİNCESS
⊙F WAПDS:

are you

able to resist?

PSYCHIC

THE PSYCHİC

says you

must keep

all your

senses alert.

PLAYING CARD

Your card is

THE SEVEN OF
DIAMONDS:

my, you're feeling

ambitious.

TEA LEAVES

AT THE BOTTOM
OF YOUR CUP

is the shape of

an umbrella:

you have more

options

than you know.

CRYSTAL BALL

According to
THE CRYSTAL
BALL,
it's never an
impossibility.

DİCE

THE DİCE

caution you
to put aside
selfish thoughts
and ask again.

ASTROLOGY

THE STARS
SAY YES—
if you will
respect yourself
in the morning.

DİCE

YOU'VE
ROLLED
SNAKE
EYES:

it's time to
settle your debts.

CRYSTAL BALL

THE
CRYSTAL
BALL

shows an

open road

ahead.

ASTROLOGY

A SOLAR ECLIPSE

hints of
an unexpected
ending.

TEA LEAVES

THE TEA
LEAVES

have taken an

oval shape:

success begins

with positive

thoughts.

PALMISTRY

According to
THE PALM
READER,
the Apollo
(ring) finger
indicates you
must gamble
to make it happen.

ASTROLOGY

THE
HEAVENLY
PLANETS

warn that the

risks are great,

but success

will be yours.

ASTROLOGY

ARIES,
the sign of the Ram,
propels you toward
a positive
outcome.

ASTROLOGY

THE
PLANETARY
FORCES

predict that

good fortune

is in store.

TAROT

THE
FOOL CARD
reminds you that
anything is
possible.

TAROT

THE
JUSTICE
CARD

is reversed:

forget about it.

PLAYING CARD

You've selected
THE ACE ⊙F
HEARTS:
a person with
the initial "A"
will make it happen.

PSYCHİC

THE PSYCHIC

advises you to

consult a

faraway relative

for advice.

TEA LEAVES

THE
TEA LEAVES
have formed
the shape of a tree:
it will come
to fruition.

DİCE

YOU'VE
ROLLED
A SEVEN,
which forecasts
frustrating delays.

ASTROLOGY

LIBRA,
the sign of the
Scales,
counsels you
to consider
another's
feelings.

CRYSTAL BALL

THE
CRYSTAL
BALL

promises the

outcome

you desire.

ASTROLOGY

VIRGO ☉,
the sign of the Virgin,
suggests you
pace yourself—
you'll get there.

PLAYING CARD

You've drawn
THE JACK OF
HEARTS:
don't plan ahead—
if it's meant to be,
it will just
happen.

TAROT

THE
CHARIOT
CARD
indicates victory

over adversity.

TAROT

THE
LOVERS
CARD

implies that you

cannot avoid it.

PALMISTRY

THE PALM
READER

sees a fork
in the life line:
you'll be happy
either way.

PLAYING CARD

You've drawn
THE TEN OF
HEARTS:
be patient
and listen.

TEA LEAVES

YOUR
TEA
LEAVES
show an anchor:
try a change
of scenery.

TAROT

THE
EMPEROR
CARD

indicates you will

overcome

several obstacles.

TAROT

THE EMPRESS
CARD

indicates the answer

will come to you

when you

least expect it.

DİCE

The dice yield
THE
NUMBER
FIVE:
you'll get what
you want
from an unknown
source.

ASTROLOGY

LEO☉,
THE SIGN
OF THE
LION☉,
urges you
to enjoy
the limelight
while it lasts.

TAROT

You've drawn

THE

HIGH

PRIESTESS

CARD:

only you can

answer this

question.

PLAYING CARD

You've drawn
THE SIX OF
HEARTS:
go for it,
but be kind to others
along the way.

PLAYING CARD

You've selected
THE FOUR
OF HEARTS:
don't be silly.

ASTROLOGY

CANCER,
THE SIGN OF
THE CRAB,

warns you

to keep your

intentions

to yourself.

DİCE

You've rolled
ПUMBER
FOUR,
which indicates
you might be unhappy
with the outcome.

ASTROLOGY

GEMINI,
THE SIGN OF
THE TWINS,

assures you

can talk

your way into it.

PLAYING CARD

You've selected
THE THREE
OF HEARTS:
it will change
your image.

TAROT

THE MAGICIAN CARD

warns that
you're taking
an unexpected
risk.

ASTROLOGY

TAURUS,
THE SIGN OF
THE BULL,
urges you to
act courageously
in the
face of adversity.

DICE

YOU'VE
ROLLED
A NINE:
yes, and you'll
be happier
for it.

TAROT

You've drawn
THE
PRINCESS OF
CUPS CARD:
wait for a secret
to be told.

PLAYING CARD

You've selected
THE KİПG
⊙F CLUBS:
it's happening
already.

CRYSTAL BALL

THE
CRYSTAL
BALL

never lies:
it's definite.

DİCE

You've rolled
ΠUMBER
FIFTEEΠ:
ask an
acquaintance—
and do
the opposite.

ASTROLOGY

THE SUN
urges you
to enjoy
the attention.

DİCE

You've
rolled a
THREE:
most
definitely.

TEA LEAVES

THE
TEA LEAVES
are in the shape
of a shell:
whatever you
desire
shall be yours.

PALMISTRY

THE PALM READER

sees an

entrepreneurial

line:

alone

you must

make it happen.

ASTROLOGY

PLU┬O

urges you to

embrace the

consequences.

DİCE

You've rolled
NUMBER
THIRTEEN:
don't
pursue it.

CRYSTAL BALL

A hazy shape

in the

CRYSTAL BALL

indicates

you're too unsure

of yourself

to proceed.

TAROT

You've drawn
THE TEΠ
⊙F CUPS:
is this what
you really
want?

ASTROLOGY

jUPiTER

gives you

the okay.

CRYSTAL BALL

THE
CRYSTAL
BALL

depicts an
empty purse:
don't
be greedy.

PALMISTRY

According to
THE PALM
READER,
the girdle of Venus
indicates you should
rely on your
imagination—
your dream
can be a reality.

TEA LEAVES

At the bottom of
YOUR
TEACUP
is a bird shape:
look outside
your
inner circle.

PLAYING CARD

The card
you've chosen is
THE
JACK OF
CLUBS:
yes, but only
with assistance
from a loved one.

TEA LEAVES

THE TEA
LEAVES
have formed
a clover:
indisputably
yes.

CRYSTAL BALL

THE
CRYSTAL
BALL

indicates that fortune
will favor you,
if you leave
the past behind.

TAROT

You've drawn
THE ACE
OF CUPS:
let someone else
take the
initiative.

PLAYING CARD

You've drawn
THE EIGHT OF
HEARTS:
you will succeed
if you use
discretion.

PSYCHIC

If today is Friday,
THE PSYCHIC
says the
answer is yes.

TAROT

You've chosen
THE TOWER
CARD:
too much pride
may prevent it
from happening.

PLAYING CARD

You've selected
THE TEN ⊙ OF
CLUBS:
it will prompt
someone from
the past to
reappear.

TEA LEAVES

THE
TEA LEAVES

appear to form

a demon:

what you want

is not what

you need.

TAROT

You've drawn
THE QUEEN OF
SWORDS:
you may have
to go it alone.

PLAYING CARD

You've selected
THE ACE OF
SPADES:
try to live
without it.

PSYCHİC

Listen to
THE PSYCHİC:
avoid it like
the plague.

PALMISTRY

THE PALM
READER
observes a
square palm
and fingers:
pay attention
to the details.

PLAYING CARD

You've drawn
THE QUEEN OF
SPADES:
look to a
dark-haired
woman
for the answer.

CRYSTAL BALL

THE
CRYSTAL
BALL

reveals a

magnifying glass:

step away and

examine your

alternatives.

TEA LEAVES

THE
TEA LEAVES

have formed
the shape of
a dollar sign:
only if you
can afford it.

DİCE

You've rolled
A TWELVE:
it will nourish
your soul.

ASTROLOGY

THE SUN,
as center of
the universe,
guarantees
you'll be
admired for
your actions.

PLAYING CARD

You've drawn

THE TEN OF SPADES:

it's not

up to you.

TAROT

You've drawn
THE KING OF
SWORDS:
someone else
will have
the last word.

PSYCHIC

THE
PSYCHIC
SAYS,
don't overlook
the details.

PALMISTRY

THE PALM
READER

sees a starred palm:

you will be

successful

by virtue

of sheer talent.

TAROT

You've drawn
THE PRINCE
OF SWORDS:
watch for
unexpected turns
in the road.

TEA LEAVES

THE
TEA LEAVES
have formed
the shape of a kite:
set your sights
even higher.

DICE

A roll of

TWELVE

means an

indisputable

yes.

ASTROLOGY

MERCURY

avows your wish

will be

granted

after

a reversal.

ASTROLOGY

PISCES,
THE SIGN OF
THE FISH,
assures that
everything
will fall
into place.

PALMISTRY

THE PALM
READER
has assessed
Chiron's bundle:
do it for
the good
of humanity.

TAROT

You've drawn
THE DEVİL
CARD:
someone is
trying to prevent
it from being so.

PLAYING CARD

You've selected
THE EİGHŤ
OF CLUBS:
you can't be
that naïve.

DICE

You've rolled

AΠ ELEVEΠ:

give it a rest.

ASTROLOGY

AQUARIUS,
the sign of the
Water Bearer,
recommends you
consider another
course of action.

TAROT

You've drawn

THE
ŦEMPERAΠCE
CARD:

yes, but

with

moderation.

TAROT

You've drawn
THE
DEATH
CARD:
what appears
to be out of reach
is anything but.

PALMISTRY

THE PALM
READER
has interpreted
Diana's arrow:
get some rest first.

DİCE

You've rolled
DOUBLE
FİVES:
await a
positive response
from a most
important
person.

ASTROLOGY

CAPRICORN,
the sign of
the Goat,
advises you to
challenge
your limits.

CRYSTAL BALL

The image in
THE CRYSTAL
BALL
is unmistakable:
you'll have
to improvise.

PLAYING CARD

You've selected
THE SEVEN
OF CLUBS:
it will help
improve
your karma.

TAROT

You've chosen

THE HANGED
MAN CARD:

yes, through

sacrifice.

TEA LEAVES

The tea leaves
form the
SHAPE ⊙F
A FİSH:
cast your
net wider.

PLAYING CARD

You've drawn
THE SIX OF
CLUBS:
it's not that
important.

TAROT

You've drawn
THE
STRENGTH
CARD:
you have the
power to
sort it out.

PALMISTRY

THE PALM
READER
has analyzed
Neptune's
rocking horse:
a change in
perspective
is in order.

PLAYING CARD

You've selected
THE FİVE ⊙F
CLUBS:
try it at
least once.

CRYSTAL BALL

IT'S CRYSTAL CLEAR:

you can

count on it.

TEA LEAVES

At the bottom
OF YOUR
TEACUP
is an image
of a bat:
meditate about it
tonight.

ASTROLOGY

SAGITTARIUS,
the sign of
the Centaur,
prompts you to forge
ahead no matter
what the cost.

PSYCHIC

Only if you want
it bad enough, says
THE PSYCHIC.

ASTROLOGY

SCORPIO,
the sign of
the Scorpion,
indicates
there's nothing
to worry about.

TEA LEAVES

Relax . . .
only then will
THE TEA
LEAVES
yield an answer.

TAROT

THE
WHEEL-OF-
FORTUNE
CARD

assures you it
will come to pass.

PLAYING CARD

The card
you've drawn is
THE FOUR ⊙ OF
CLUBS:
a change
is in the making.

PALMISTRY

THE PALM
READER
observes a
mystic cross
in the palm:
have faith.

TAROT

THE
HERMIT
CARD

urges you
to look
inward first.

DİCE

You've rolled
AN EIGHT,
which indicates
that someone
is pressuring you.
Push them back.

PLAYING CARD

THE QUEEN OF HEARTS

urges you to follow
your heart instead
of what others say.

PALMISTRY

THE PALM READER

sees a butterfly shape

in the hand:

rely on the

help of

a stranger.

PSYCHIC

THE PSYCHIC

indicates yes,
but be on guard
against the
selfishness
of others.

TAROT

You've drawn
THE ACE ⊙F
WAΠDS.
Do you have
to be in charge?
If not,
step aside.

PLAYING CARD

Your card is the
SİX ⊙F
DİAM⊙ΠDS:
have a
good cry first.

TEA LEAVES

THE TEA LEAVES

have formed
a mushroom shape;
try to look at it
through the eyes
of a child.

PALMISTRY

According to
THE PALM
READER,
the Saturn (middle)
finger
indicates a
guilty conscience—
apologize first.

PSYCHİC

THE
PSYCHIC'S
answer is
plain and simple:
no.

TAROT

You've drawn
THE KİΠG
⊙F CUPS:
the answer will
come to you
naturally.

PALMISTRY

According to
THE PALM
READER,
the Jupiter (index)
finger indicates
you need to
tone it down.

DĬCE

THE DİCE

have rolled

off the table:

let it go.

ASTROLOGY

A LUNAR ECLIPSE

indicates uncertainty—
reconsider your
question
and ask again.

CRYSTAL BALL

THE
CRYSTAL
BALL

predicts you'll

get a lucky

break.

PLAYING CARD

THE FIVE OF DIAMONDS

indicates an

unequivocal yes.

PALMISTRY

According to
THE PALM
READER,
the life line
shows incredible
fortitude:
be patient.

PSYCHIC

THE PSYCHIC

advises you to

make an offer

and see

what happens.

TAROT

You've drawn
THE QUEEN
OF CUPS:
your present goal
is unreachable.

PSYCHIC

THE PSYCHIC

senses you are

not yet ready

for the answer.

TEA LEAVES

A windmill
has appeared
among the
TEA LEAVES:
the situation will
change drastically
before it's resolved.

PSYCHİC

THE PSYCHİC

has spoken:

not this year.

ASTROLOGY

THE STARS
urge you not
to delay.

DİCE

A ROLL
OF SIXTEEN

reveals the answer is yes,

but only if you

get to it

immediately.

CRYSTAL BALL

According to
THE CRYSTAL
BALL,
a negative force
is keeping you
from success.

PALMISTRY

THE PALM
READER
sees a crescent
in the hand:
act as if it's
already
happened.

TAROT

You've drawn
THE PRİⴑCE
⊙F CUPS:
yes, with the help
of a man
who's not afraid
of his
feminine side.

PLAYING CARD

You've selected the
THREE OF
DIAMONDS:
nothing ventured,
nothing gained.

PSYCHIC

THE PSYCHIC

says to expect

your answer

to emerge

during a crisis.

CRYSTAL BALL

According to

THE CRYSTAL
BALL,

someone else

has already made

the decision

for you.

TEA LEAVES

A flower
has appeared
among the
TEA LEAVES:
take a fresh
approach.

ASTROLOGY

MARS,
the planet of war,
urges you
to go after
what you desire.

TAROT

You've drawn
THE ACE OF
PENTACLES:
you will be rewarded
for your efforts.

PSYCHIC

THE PSYCHIC

says, sooner

than you know.

PLAYING CARD

You've drawn the
THREE OF
SPADES:
the answer to your
question
is a resounding yes.

PALMISTRY

THE PALM READER

sees a curving
marriage line:
the circumstances
will change
for the better.

TEA LEAVES

THE TEA
LEAVES
have formed the
shape of a snake:
things are not
as they appear.

CRYSTAL BALL

THE
CRYSTAL
BALL

shows a

closed door:

is something

holding

you back?

DICE

You've rolled
THE NUMBER
FOURTEEN:
a friend's help
will get you
through.

ASTROLOGY

JUPITER,
the planet of
abundance,
blesses you with
a yes answer.

CRYSTAL BALL

THE
CRYSTAL
BALL'S

answer:

more than you

can imagine.

ASTROLOGY

THE PLANET SATURN

indicates there's
turbulence
ahead if you do.

DİCE

You've rolled
DOUBLE SIXES:
fortune is
favoring you,
so seize
the moment.

TAROT

You've drawn
THE KİΠG ☉F
WAΠDS:
only if you
can maintain
control.

PSYCHIC

THE PSYCHIC

senses it's
already in
the works.

PLAYING CARD

THE ACE OF
DIAMONDS

forecasts success

if you act

immediately.

TEA LEAVES

THE
TEA LEAVES
have formed
an anchor shape:
assess your
financial situation
first.

PALMISTRY

THE PALM
READER

sees dual

affection lines:

you can't

have it

both ways.

CRYSTAL BALL

THE
CRYSTAL
BALL

assures you will
gain that which
you seek.

PALMISTRY

THE PALM READER

has assessed
Diana's bow:
listen to your
hunches.

DİCE

You've rolled
ΝUΜBER ΤΕΝ:
you will obtain
what you
wish for.

ASTROLOGY

URANUS,
the planet of
revolution,
says yes, but it will
change your
life forever.

CRYSTAL BALL

According to
THE
CRYSTAL
BALL,
you may
rely on it.

TAROT

You've drawn
THE QUEEN
OF WANDS:
don't bite the
hand that
feeds you.

PSYCHİC

THE
PSYCHIC
SENSES
you're about to
encounter a
fork in the road:
stick to the
well-trodden path.

CRYSTAL BALL

THE CRYSTAL
BALL

shows a sand castle:

don't forget to

enjoy yourself.

DICE

You've rolled
ΠUMBER FIVE:
learn from the
lessons of
the past.

PLAYING CARD

You've drawn
THE SIX OF
SPADES:
not with
that attitude.

TAROT

You've drawn
THE PRINCESS
OF SWORDS:
keen judgment
is required.

ABOUT THE AUTHOR

GEORGIA ROUTSIS SAVAS has been divining in some shape or form for as long as she can remember. ∞ Her broad-ranging career has taken her from composing advertising copy for *Ms.* magazine to writing fashion reports for CNN's hit show *Style With Elsa Klensch.* ∞ She writes a popular monthly horoscope column for *In Style* magazine, and in the past has written astro forecasts for an array of national magazines, including *Child, The New York Daily News Sunday Magazine* and *Sassy.* ∞ She is the author of one book, *Seventeen* magazine's *Total Astrology: What the Stars Say about Life and Love.* ∞ She also does private consultations, chart mapping and cosmic divination. ∞ These days, she gazes at the stars from her home on the North Carolina coast.